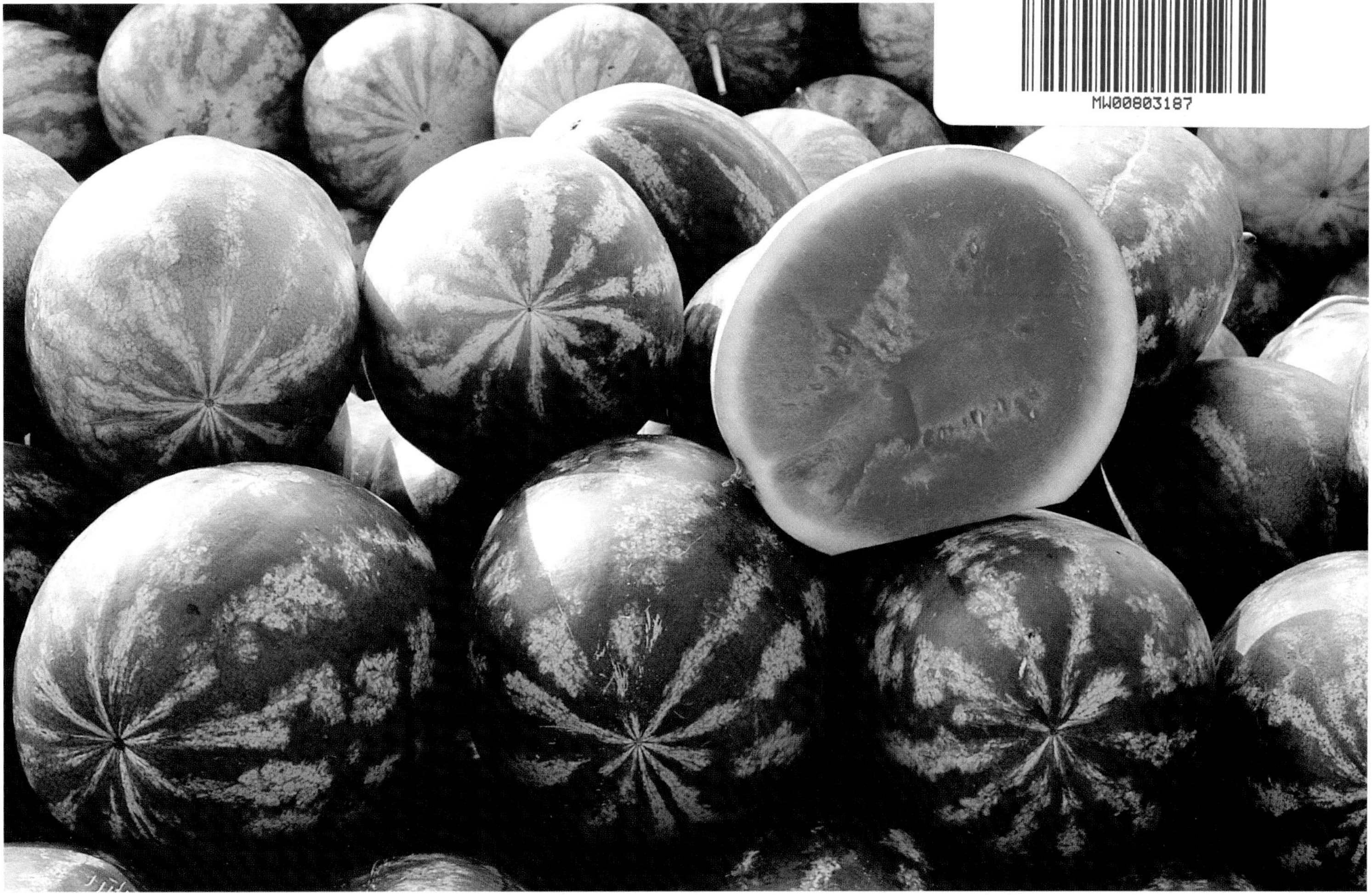

watermelons

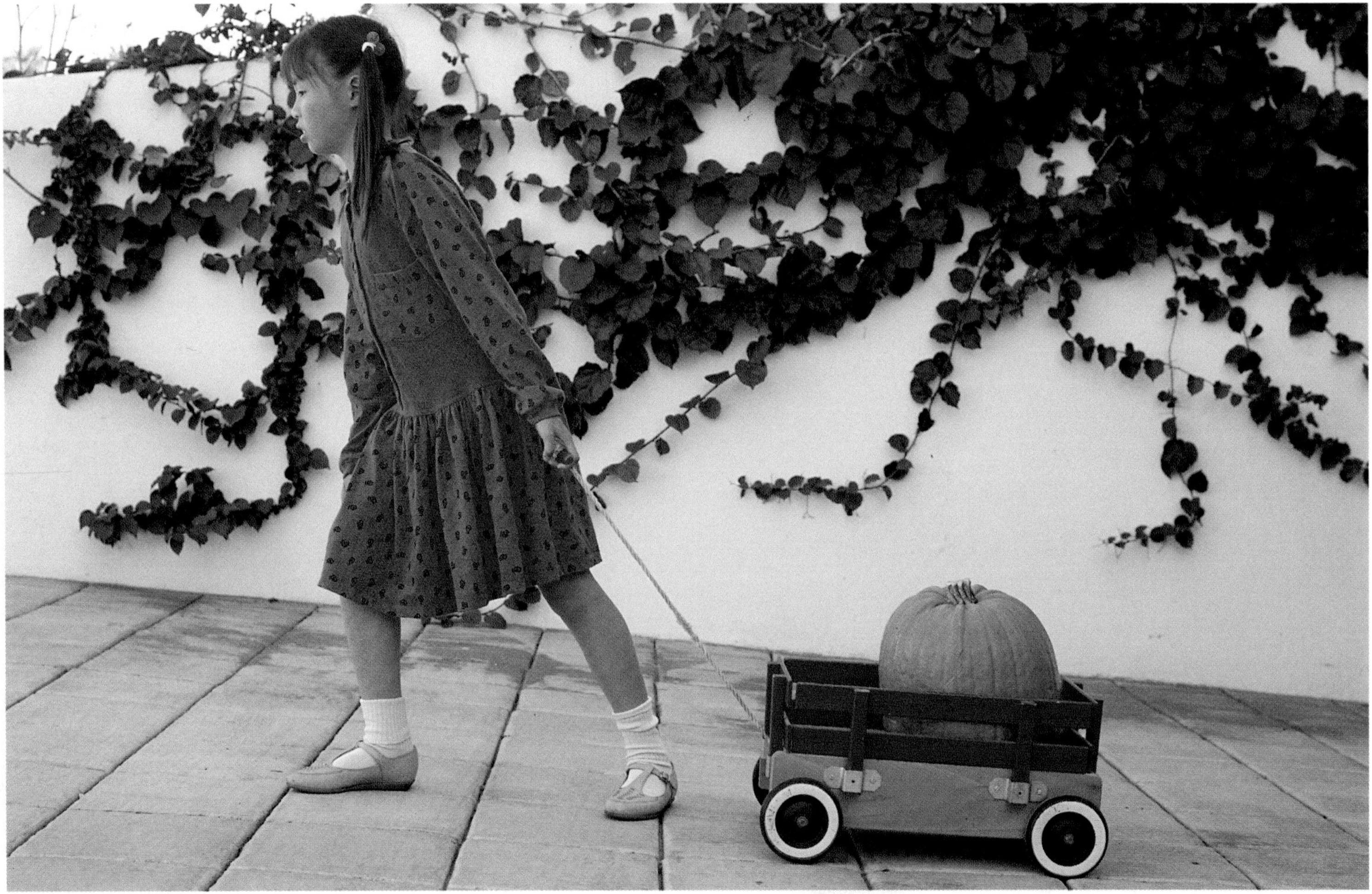

wagon

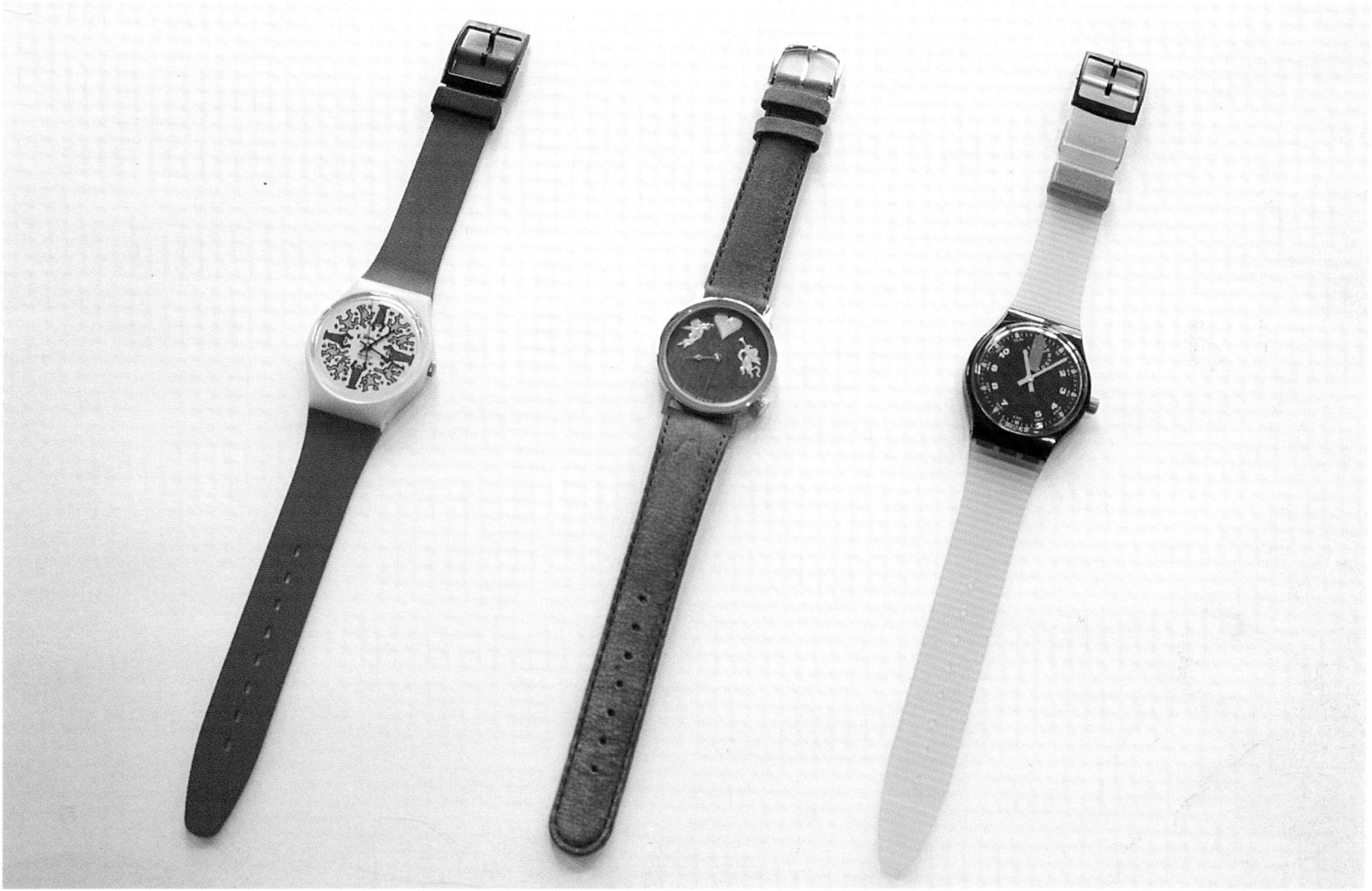

watches

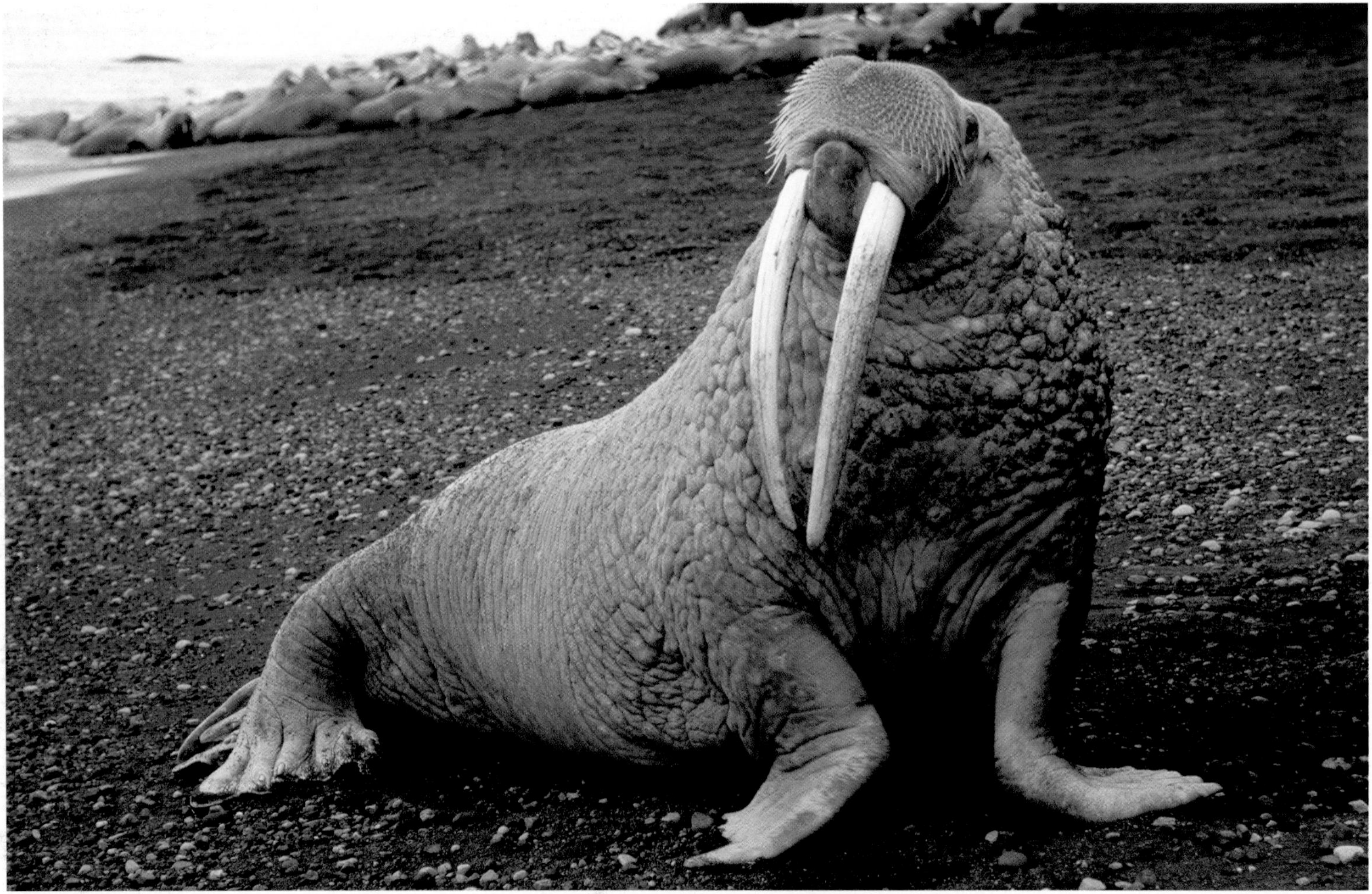

walrus

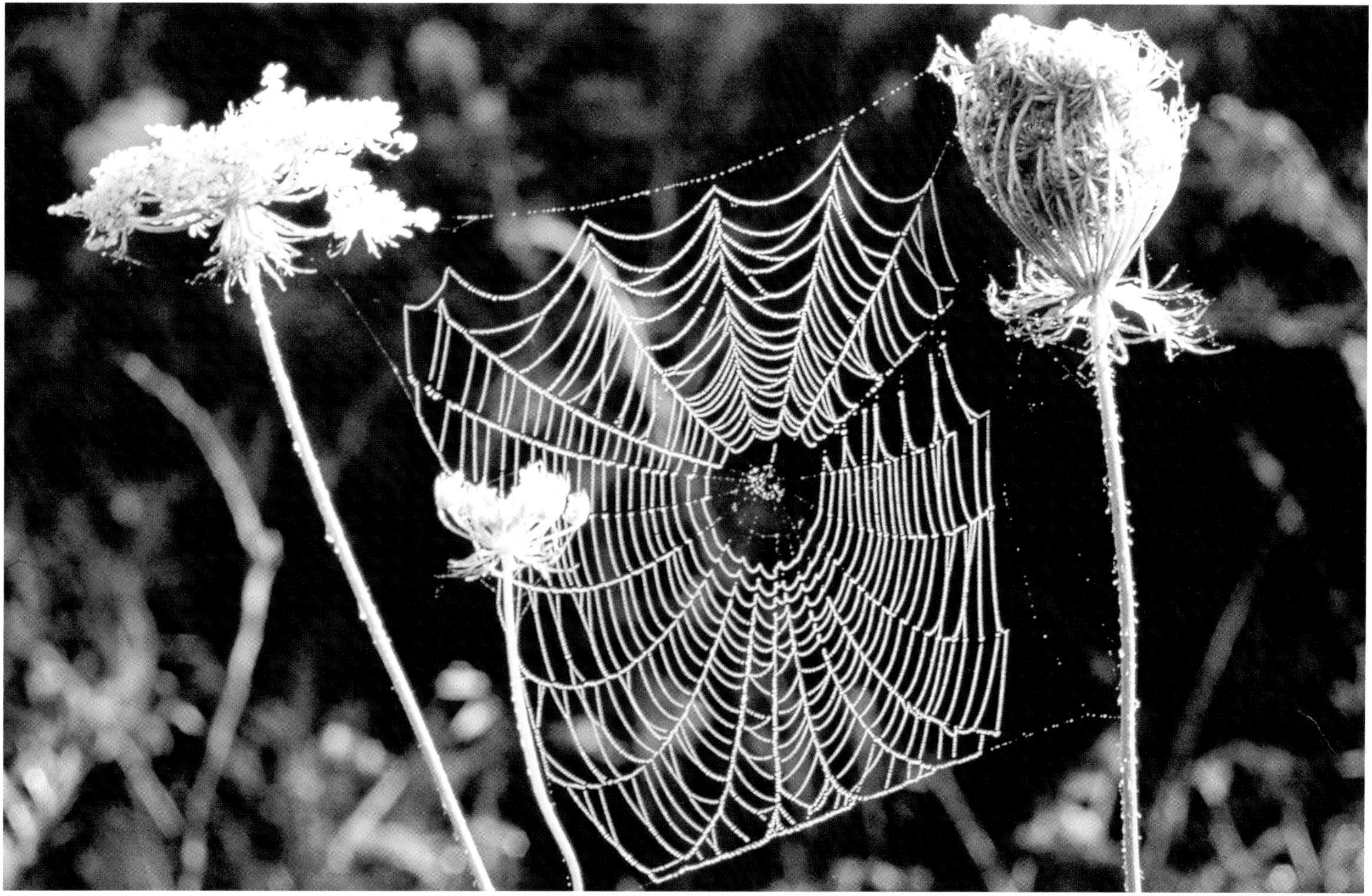

web

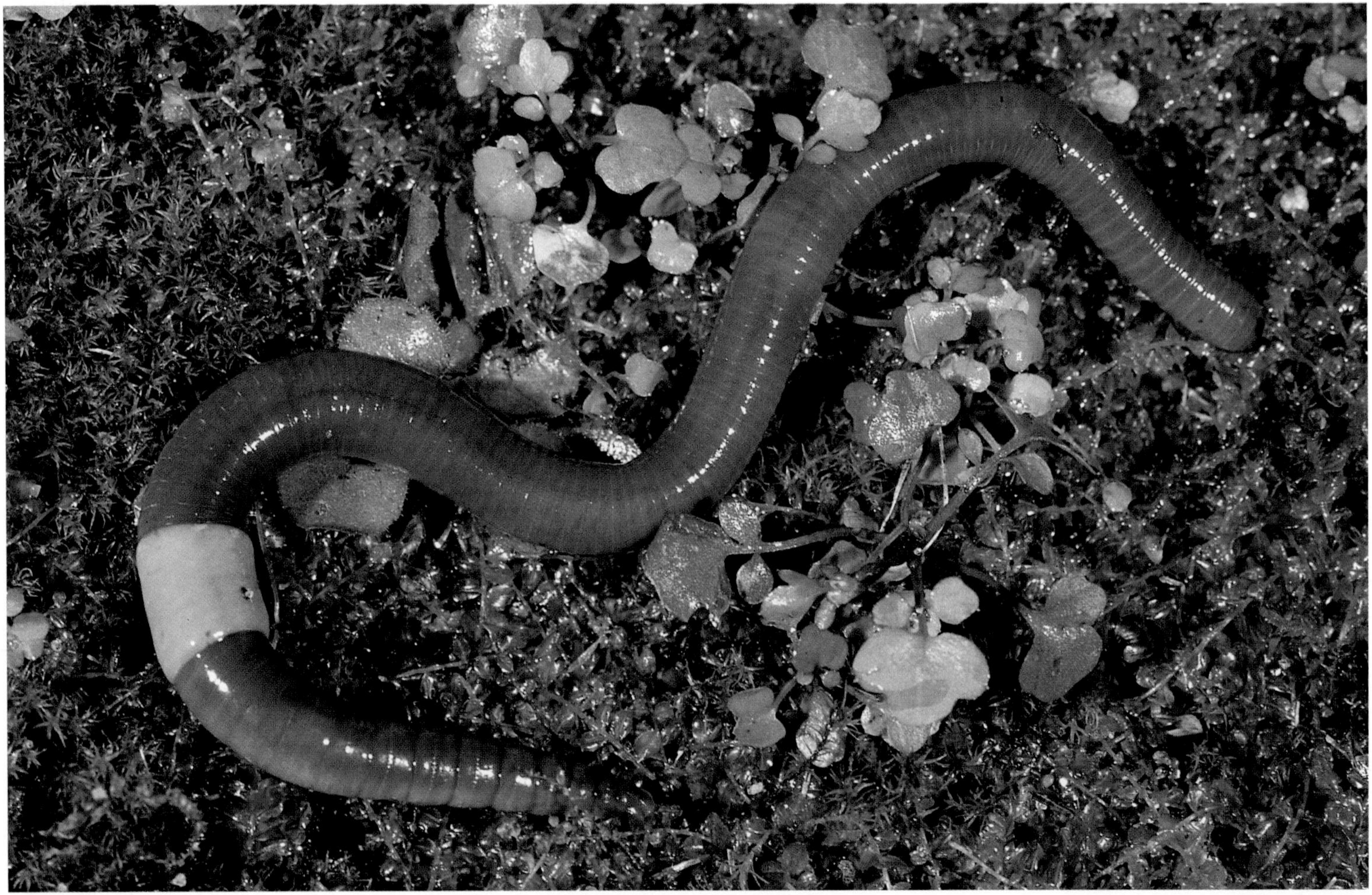

worm

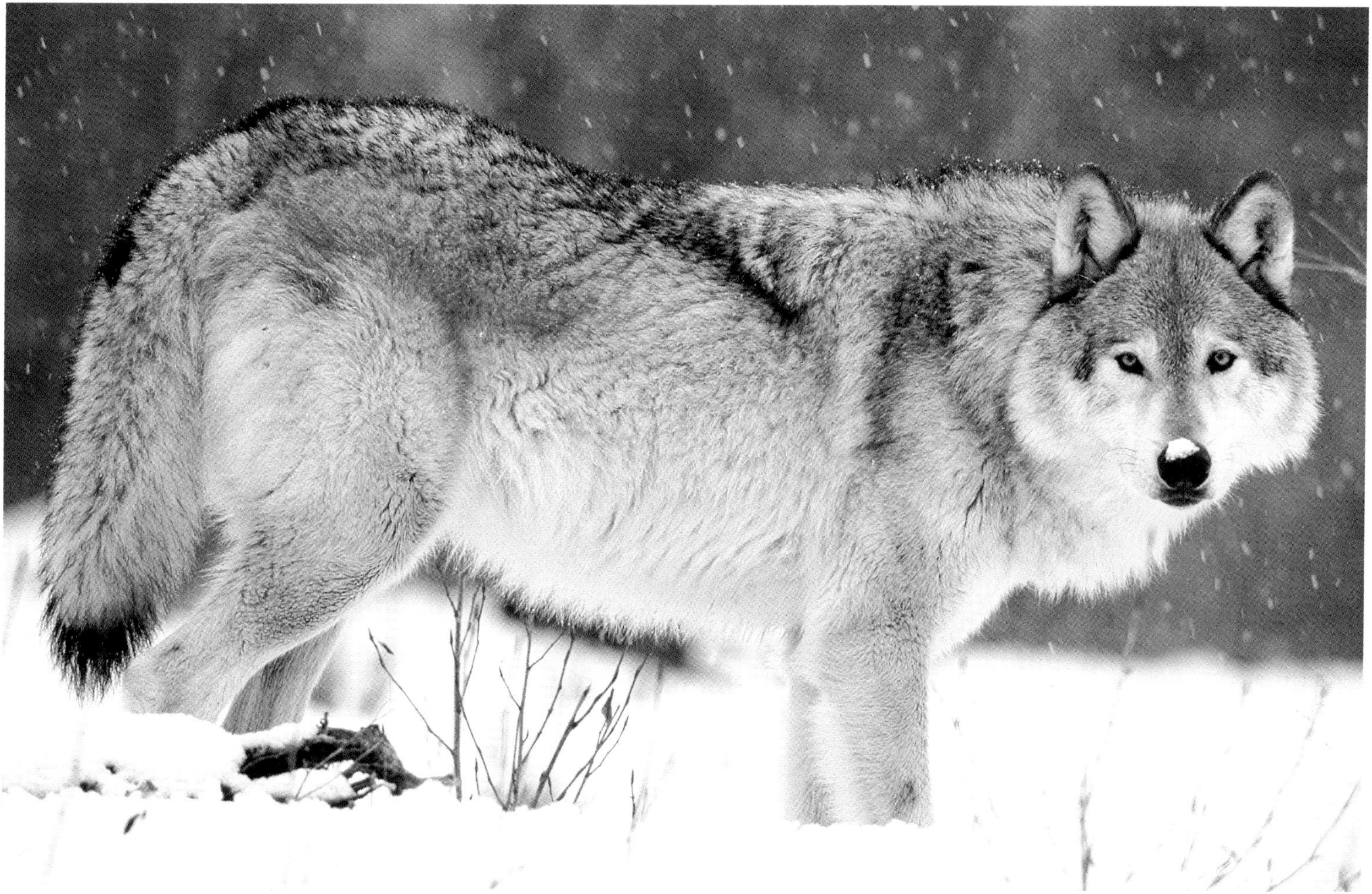

wolf

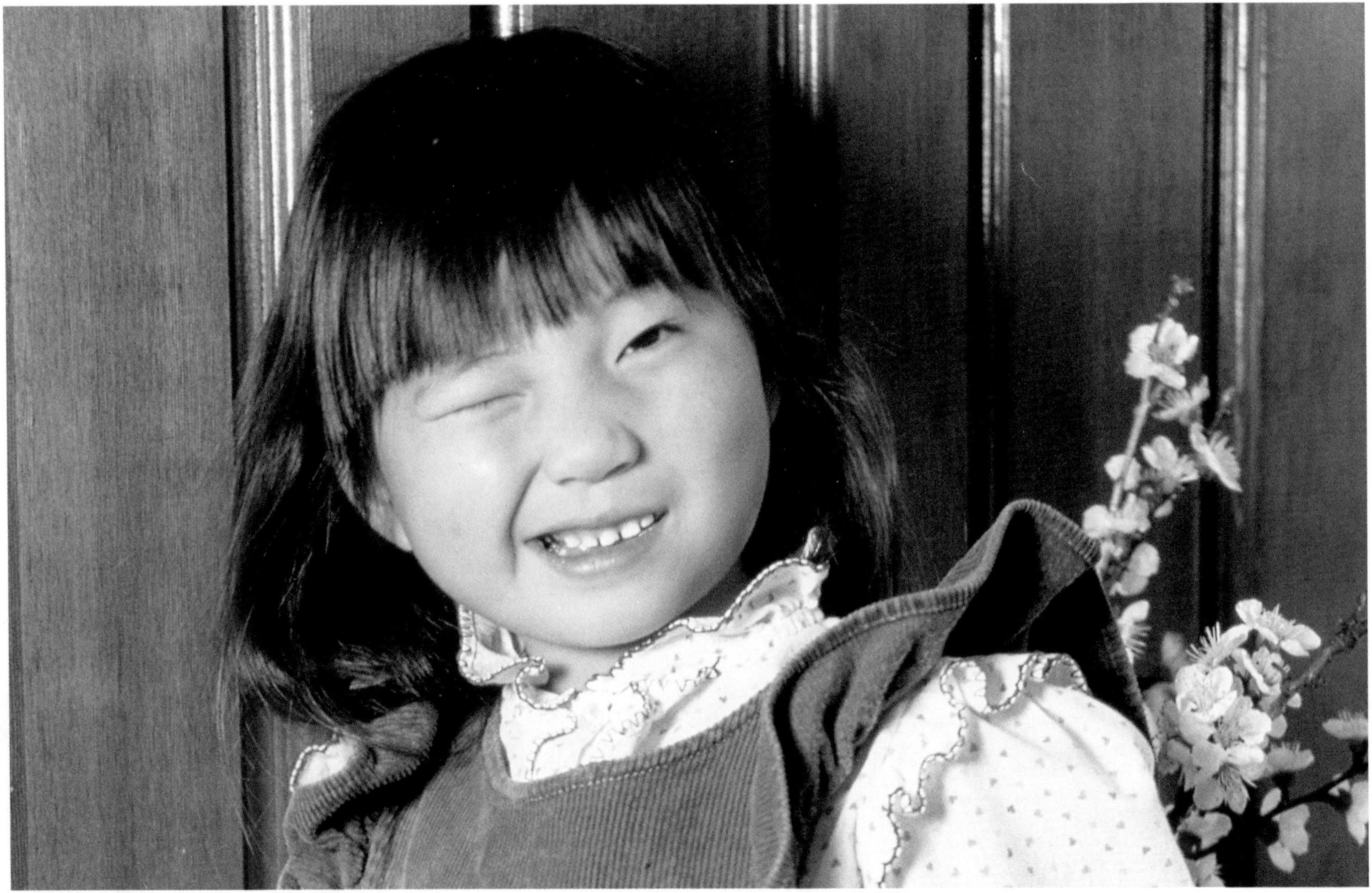

wink